My First Book about the Animal Alphabet of Australia

Amazing Animal Books Children's Picture Books

By Molly Davidson

Mendon Cottage Books

JD-Biz Publishing

Read More Amazing Animal Books

Purchase at Amazon.com

Download Free Books!
http://MendonCottageBooks.com

 **is for a Sea Anemone.**

Sea anemones live in the Great Barrier Reef off the shores of Australia.

They are predator animals, as fish swim by venom is inject into their prey paralyzes them so the anemone can eat them.

 is for a Brushtail Possum.

Brushtail possums are marsupials that live in Australia and are not related to opossums that live in North America.

They are the largest possums, they can stand over 3 feet tall.

C is for a Dingo, which has the scientific name of Canis Lupus Dingo.

They live in the mountains, tropical forests, and deserts of Australia.

Dingoes hunt at night, usually in packs. They attack large prey, like kangaroos.

D is for a Weedy Sea Dragon.

They swim off the southern coast of Australia.

Weedy sea dragons just float slowly with the water, using their camouflage as protection.

They have no teeth, and eat tiny zooplankton.

 **is for an Emu.**

The emu can be found all over Australia, and is also on the coat of arms for Australia.

Emus are the second largest birds, standing up to 6 1/2 feet tall.

E is for an Echidna. (*Bonus E)

They live on the coast and highlands of Australia.

Their spikes have muscles, like a porcupine, making it so the echidna can control them.

 **is for an Eastern Banjo Frog.**

Fir0002/Flagstaffotos © <u>Wikimedia Commons</u>

It is only found in Eastern Australia.

They will burrow in the mud when it is dry or too hot, then will come back out after it rains.

Adults are about 7 - 8 cm (3 inches) long.

G is for Goanna.

Goanna's live all over Australia, except Tasmania.

They use their large, sharp teeth and claws to eat snakes, lizards, birds, and eggs.

A goanna can stand and run on its back feet, as well as climb trees.

 is for a Humpback Whale.

They spend the summers in the warm oceans around Asia and Australia.

Humpback whales can be up to 65 feet long, that's one and a half school buses!

I is for an Isoodon Macrourus, the scientific name for the Northern Brown Bandicoot.

It lives in eucalypt forests in northern Australia.

Baby bandicoots are only in their mother for 12 days before they are born.

They eat insects, spiders, berries, worms, fungus, roots of plants, and grass seed.

 **is for a Box Jellyfish.**

Peter Southwood © <u>Wikimedia Commons</u>

The box jellyfish lives in Australia's northern oceans.

They are the most venomous marine animal that we know of; their string is almost always fatal.

K  is for a Koala.

Koalas are a marsupial (not a bear) that lives in forests throughout Australia.

They are mostly active at night, and they sleep 18 - 20 hours per day.

L is for a Blue - Tongued Lizard.

Rod Waddington © <u>Wikimedia Commons</u>

Most of them live on the savannahs of Australia.

They use their blue tongues to confuse their predators into thinking they are dangerous.

M is for Murray Cod.

Codman © <u>Wikimedia Commons</u>

Murray cod are the largest fish living in the freshwaters of Australia.

They will eat anything they can fit in their mouths; fish, yabbies, crayfish, shrimp, muscles, waterfowl, and tortoises.

 **is for a Numbat.**

![Numbat]

Numbats are marsupials that live in southern Australia, but they are quickly becoming extinct.

They eat mostly termites, ants, and insects.

O

is for Ornithorhynchus Anatinus, the scientific name for a Platypus.

Stefan Craft © <u>Wikimedia Commons</u>

The only live on the east side of Australia and Tasmania.

Platypuses are bottom feeders, they scoop up worms, shellfish, and larvae, then go to the surface to eat.

 **is for a Pademelon.**

PanBK © <u>Wikimedia Commons</u>

They live in the coasts of Australia, Papua New Guinea, and Tasmania.

Pademelon's eat at night, when it is cool. They eat leaves, berries, herbs, and grasses.

Q is for a Spotted Quoll.

Ways © <u>Wikimedia Commons</u>

They live in the forests of Australia, New Guinea, and Tasmania.

Quolls are marsupials, they give birth to up to 30 tiny babies, that they keep save in their pouch.

 **is for a Red Kangaroo.**

A baby kangaroo is called a joey. Is it only about the size of a lima bean when it is born.

The red kangaroo is the national animal of Australia.

S is for a Saltwater Crocodile.

jemasmith © Wikimedia Commons

They live in the oceans north of Australia.

They are the largest crocodiles; they can be as long as 17 feet and weigh up to 1,000 pounds.

Saltwater crocodiles live for about 70 years.

T is for a Tasmanian Devil.

Tasmanian devils are marsupials that only live in Tasmania, an island of Australia.

They see the best when something is moving in the dark.

They are scavengers, eating meat of dead animals, their favorite are wombats.

 **is for a Sea Urchin.**

They live in the warm waters of the Barrier Reef.

Sea urchins are the longest living animal, up to 200 years in the wild.

They have 5 sharp teeth, on the bottom side, which can drill holes in rocks.

V

is for a Vombatus Ursinus, the scientific name for a Wombat.

Wombats are marsupials that live in the forests on the coast of Australia.

They have sharp claws and short legs that are perfect for digging burrows.

 **is for a Spotted Wobbegong.**

Taso Viglas © <u>Wikimedia Commons</u>

They are carpet sharks that live on the ocean bottoms around Australia and Indonesia.

Wobbegong means shaggy beard, because they have stripes of skin on their faces, like a beard.

X is for Xylotrupes Ulysses, which is the scientific name for a Rhinoceros Beetle.

Bernard DUPONT © Wikimedia Commons

They live on the coasts of Queensland, Australia.

The boys use their horn to fight for the girls.

Y

is for a Yellow-Tailed Black Cockatoo.

Bronwyn Scanlon © <u>Wikimedia Commons</u>

They can be found in south-eastern Australia.

These cockatoos are the longest in Australia; they can be up to 25 1/2 inches long.

Z is for a Flower Spider, whose scientific name is Zygometis Lactea.

Flower spiders camouflage with the flowers so they can ambush their prey.

The boys have dark bands on their legs.

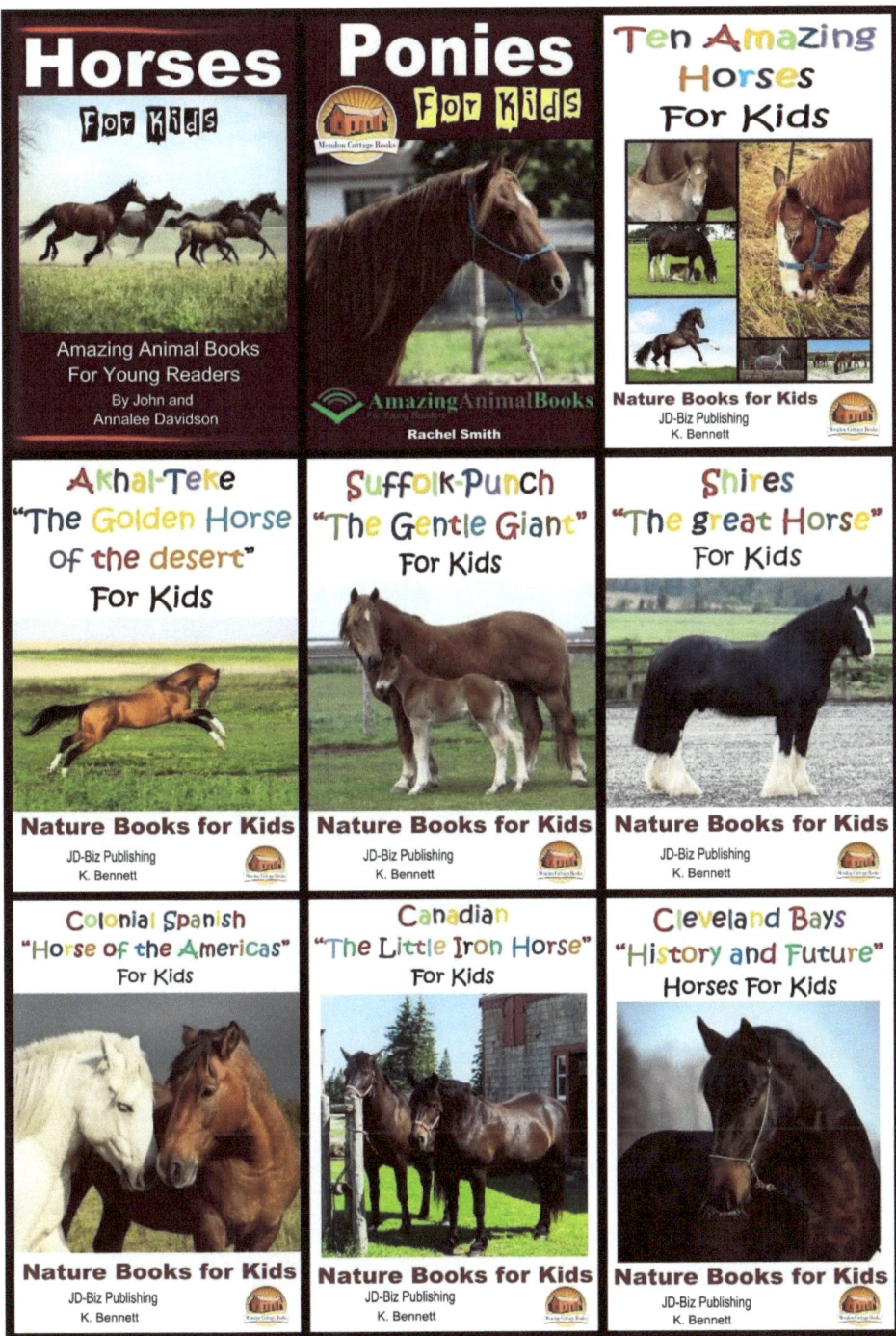

Our books are available at

1. Amazon.com

2. Barnes and Noble

3. Itunes

4. Kobo

5. Smashwords

6. Google Play Books

Download Free Books!
http://MendonCottageBooks.com

Publisher

JD-Biz Corp

P O Box 374

Mendon, Utah 84325

http://www.jd-biz.com/

Mendon Cottage Books

P O Box 374, Mendon Utah 84325